What Living Things Need

Water

Vic Parker

www.raintreepublishers.co.uk

Visit our website to find out more information about **Raintree** books.

To order:

☎ Phone 44 (0) 1865 888112

▤ Send a fax to 44 (0) 1865 314091

💻 Visit the Raintree Bookshop at **www.raintreepublishers.co.uk** to browse our catalogue and order online.

First published in Great Britain by Raintree, Halley Court, Jordan Hill, Oxford OX2 8EJ, part of Harcourt Education.
Raintree is a registered trademark of Harcourt Education Ltd.

Editorial: Jilly Attwood and Kathy Peltan
Design: Jo Hinton-Malivoire and Bigtop
Picture Research: Ruth Blair and Andrea Sadler
Production: Séverine Ribierre

Originated by Modern Age House Ltd, Hong Kong
Printed and bound in China by South China Printing Company

10 digit ISBN 1 406 20035 2
13 digit ISBN 978 1 406 20035 5

10 09 08 07 06
10 9 8 7 6 5 4 3 2 1

British Library Cataloguing in Publication Data
Parker, Victoria
Water. – (What living things need)
572.5'39
A full catalogue record for this book is available from the British Library.

Acknowledgements
The publishers would like to thank the following for permission to reproduce photographs: Alamy Images pp. **7** (Papillo), **11** (Stock Connection Distribution), back cover (tiger, Papillo); Corbis pp. **4**, **9** (Richard T. Nowitz), **23** (thirsty, Richard T. Nowitz); FLPA pp. **10** (S. McCutcheon), **17** (Silvestris), **19** (Minden Pictures), back cover (dolphins, Minden Pictures); Getty Images pp. **21** (Photodisc), **22** (Digital Vision), **23** (desert, Photodisc); Harcourt Education Ltd pp. **12**, **13** (Chris Honeywell), **14**, **23**, (roots) **23** (seed); Harcourt Education Ltd (Tudor Photography) pp. **5**, **6**, **22**, **23** (liquid); NHPA pp. **15** (R. Sorensen & J. Olsen) **16** (Martin Harvey), **18** (Laurie Campbell), **20** (Mike Lane); TopFoto pp. **8** (Sean Cayton, The Image Works).

Cover photograph reproduced with permission of Getty Images.

The publishers would like to thank Michael Scott for his assistance in the preparation of this book.

Every effort has been made to contact copyright holders of any material reproduced in this book. Any omissions will be rectified in subsequent printings if notice is given to the publishers.

The paper used to print this book comes from sustainable resources.

Contents

Some words are shown in bold, **like this**. You can find them in the picture glossary on page 23.

What is a living thing?

Living things are things that grow.

People, animals, and plants are living things.

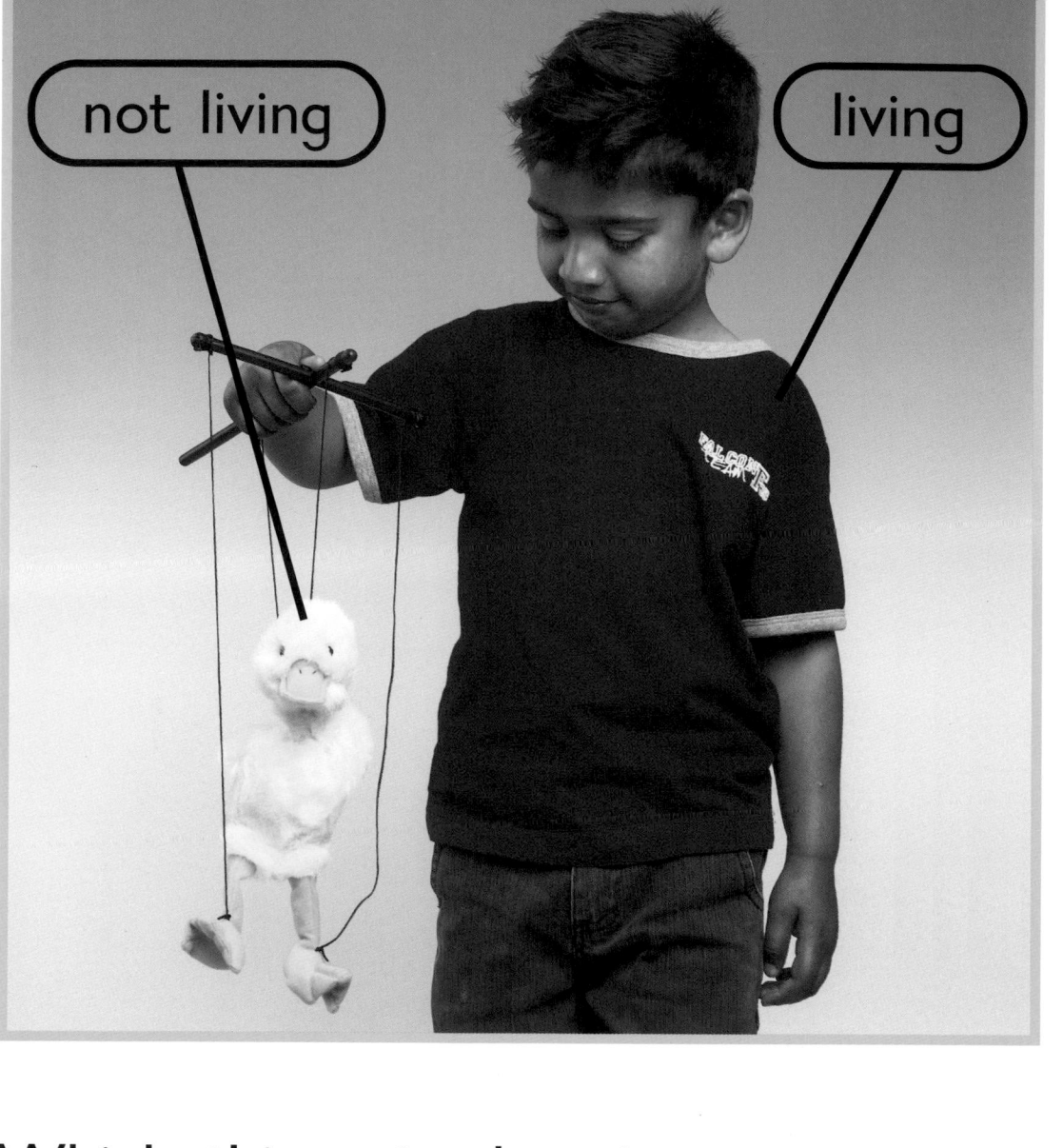

Which things in the picture are living and which are not?

What is water?

Water is a **liquid**.

You can see through water. Water has no smell or taste.

All living things need water.

Why do we need water?

We need water to drink.

You need water to move, talk, think, and grow.

If we do not drink water, we get **thirsty** and feel ill.

Where does water come from?

clouds

rain

Water falls from clouds as rain.

Rain fills up rivers, lakes,
and the sea.

Pipes bring clean water to our homes and gardens.

Do plants need water?

Plants need water to grow.

Fill a few pots with soil.
Plant a **seed** into each pot.

Water some pots every day but
do not water the others.

Which seeds do you think
will grow?

Where do plants get water from?

Most plants have **roots** under the soil.

The roots take in rain that falls onto the soil.

These plants have long roots in the water.

The roots take in the pond water.

Do animals need water?

Animals need to drink water too.

Some animals like to wash
with water!

Some animals find their food
in water.

This bird needs to live near water.

What needs a lot of water?

Some animals need to keep wet all the time.

This toad lives near a pond so it can keep wet.

These dolphins live in seawater all
the time.

What needs little water?

Camels do not have to drink very often.

A camel can store water in its body.

Cactus plants do not need much water.

They live in the **desert** where it hardly ever rains.

Can you guess?

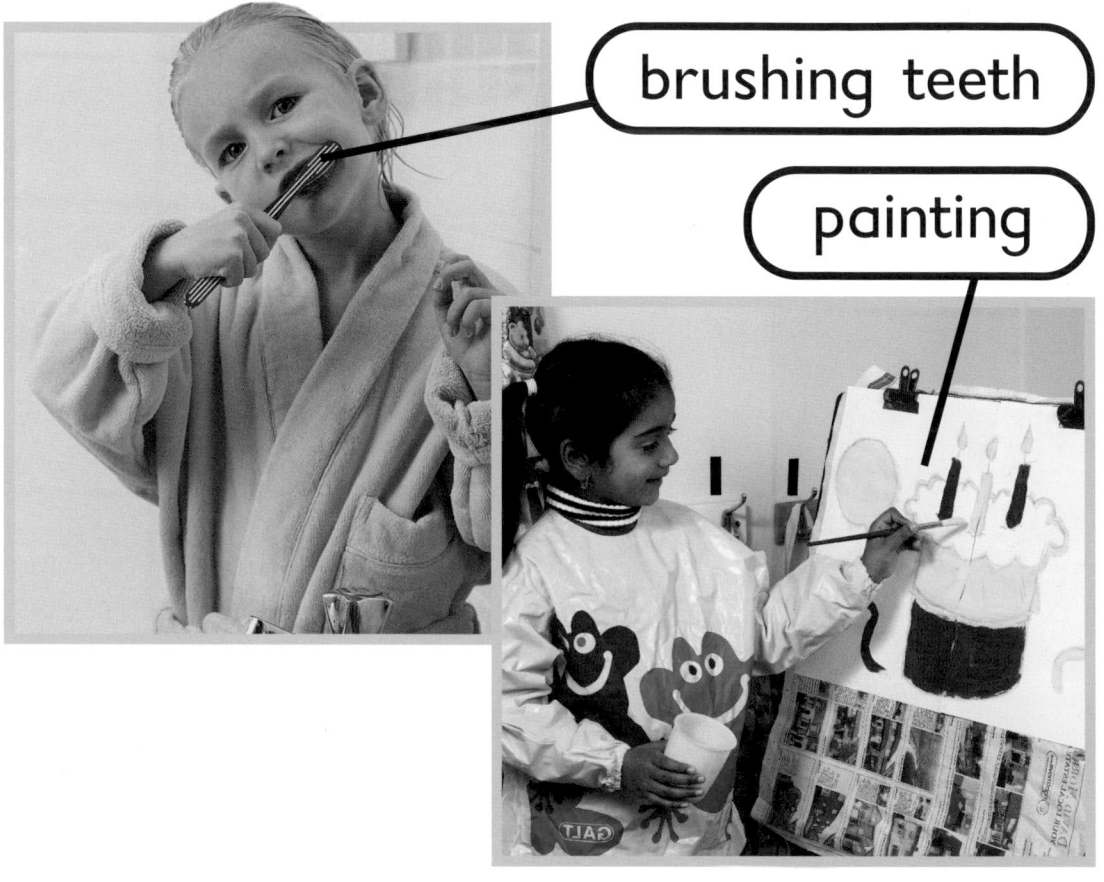

brushing teeth

painting

People must have water for drinking.

What else do people need
water for?

Glossary

 **desert** a hot, dry, sandy place where it hardly ever rains

 **liquid** something runny that you can pour, like water or milk

 **roots** part of a plant that sucks up water

 **seed** a hard, ball-shaped part of a plant that grows into a new plant

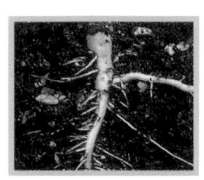 **thirsty** feeling as though you badly need a drink